The Art of Academic Advising – The Five-Step Process
– Community\Technical College Edition

By Dr. Jeffrey C. Hoffman

Copyright © 2018, Jeffrey C. Hoffman

All rights reserved.

No part of this book may be used

Or reproduced in any manner whatsoever

Without the written permission of the Publisher.

Printed in the United States of America.

Library of Congress Cataloging-in-Publication Data

Hoffman, Jeffrey C.

The art of academic advising – The Five-Step Process – Community\Technical College Edition / Dr. Jeffrey C. Hoffman.

Seventh Printing

Includes bibliographical references.

ISBN #: 9781726342360
Cover Design: D. Natasha Ferguson-Hoffman

1. Academic advising. 2. Student Advising. 3. Purposeful Advising

FIRST EDITION

Dedication

This book is dedicated to all of these hard-working academic advisors in the colleges whose role is to help each student forge a path of academic success to finish their course of instruction in a timely and successful manner.

This book is also dedicated to the most important people on the college campus – the students!

My hopes and prayer are that this book provides the academic advisor a simple framework for taking care of these students and in so doing - change lives one person at a time.

Acknowledgements

I could not have written this book without the amazing editing help of Julie Floyd and Dr. Dahlia Allen and the valuable publishing guidance of Dr. Morris Clarington and Mr. Sam Lester. Thanks to my beautiful and very patient wife – Jeni. Waggonner Hoffman. I want to thank Dr. Rich Turner for his insight on academic advising in the college and university settings. I'm also eternally grateful to my Central Georgia Technical College family that make-up some of the best academic advisors on the planet. I have learned so much from you. Thank God for His love and mercy.

Table of Contents

Part One: Introduction & Purposeful Advisement

Chapter I – Introduction to *The Art of Academic Advising*..2

Chapter II - The Five Axioms of Purposeful Advisement……………………………....………….13

Chapter III – To the reader……………………....……18

Chapter IV - Axiom #1 – Be academically prepared for the chosen coursework within a program of study…………………………………….….………….22

Chapter V – Specifics to Check for Academic Preparedness ………………………………….....…………….……29

Chapter VI - Axiom #2 – Be physically prepared for chosen coursework……………………………….……32

Chapter VII– Check for Physical Preparedness……….37

Chapter VIII - Axiom #3 – Be financially capable of paying for the chosen coursework………………..…….40

Chapter IX – Specific Points of Financial Preparedness……………………………….……….43

Chapter X - Axiom #4 – Be advised with graduation in mind-Every time……………………...……….………48

Chapter XI - Axiom #5 – Be registered! …………….....54

Part Two: Academic Advising Scenarios

Chapter XII - Scenario #1

    Advising One-On-One……………………...……..57

Chapter XIII - Scenario #2

    Advising One-On-One – Failed MATH 1111……..…63

Chapter XIV - Scenario #3

    Advising an Online Student…………………….....70

Chapter XV - Scenario #4

    Advising a Student that's "Undecided"…………….75

Part Three: Questions on Purposeful Academic Advising

Chapter XVI – Question #1 - How long does it normally take to go through all these points with a student? ………………………………………………………….82

Chapter XVII – Question #2 - Do program advisors have to advise the same way that academic advisors in Student Services do? ……………………………….……83

Chapter XVIII - Question #3 - Isn't vocational or technical college student advisement different from liberal arts college student advisement? …...………….84

Chapter XIX – Question #4 - Isn't all this what is supposed to be covered in New Student Orientation? ………………………………………………..………….88

Chapter XX – Question #5 - Where can I find more resources and organizations that I can contact for more information about other aspects of academic advisement? ……………………………………….………..………90

Chapter XXI - Central Georgia Technical College Five-Step ALFAA Advisement Plan………………..……93

Chapter XXII – Addressing the Horror Stories……………………………….…... ………102
.
Epilogue…………..…………………………………..…..…..114

Part One: Introduction & Purposeful Advisement

Chapter I

Introduction to the *Art of Academic Advising*

I am thrilled with the prospect that with this book I can share the simple secrets at the heart of academic advising. The inspiration for this book came from the thousands of students that I have encountered over the past decade and a half and the thrill of watching them leave our college and move into a career that allows them to make a comfortable living wage. But a bigger inspiration for writing this book has been the distressing reality that bad advising has slowed student progress.

It has caused students to stop coming to class and even to drop out of school and abandon their dreams. These are *horror stories* playing out right in front of our faces, and we don't even see it as students drop out or quit coming to class. How distressing are these horror stories? Consider the following common scenarios in any college:

Stephanie, a pre-nursing student, ...

...was misadvised by being scheduled into too many classes and being unable to handle the course load. She failed one of those classes, a course required for the nursing program she hoped to enter. In reality, nursing programs are competitive with limited admissions. Failing that required class caused Stephanie's GPA to drop. She had no chance of entering the nursing program. Her hopes were dashed, and she had no confidence to retake the necessary course. She dropped out of college.

DeShaun is a cosmetology major…

…in his first-semester courses. He showed up for class on the first day of the semester. The instructor told the class that each student needed an additional mannequin kit for his class. DeShaun went to the bookstore to purchase the needed kit, but the people running the bookstore said that he didn't have any financial aid from which to purchase it. He dropped the class because he didn't have the funds to buy the $200.00 cosmetology kit. This lack of money put DeShaun off track to finish his program. The cosmetology courses are sequenced, and he would have to wait another full year to try the program again.

Belle is a political science major…

…in the second semester of her sophomore year. She had always told herself that she wasn't a math person, but she finally found the courage to enroll in her required college algebra class. She stayed up late working long hours at night on her math and got up early in the morning to do more of her homework but to no avail. She asked her poly sci friends to help her, but they weren't comfortable with math either. With a total lack of confidence and nowhere to turn, she failed the course. Belle was devastated because failing this class caused her GPA to drop below the requirement for her scholarship. Without her scholarship, Belle could not pay additional tuition and had to turn to her parents for college money. Once proud of her progress and her scholarship, Belle was devastated.

Matt is an online student…

…and an enthusiastic gamer. He lives in his parents' basement, and his parents' condition for living with them is that he must enroll in community college. They want him to find an area of interest that will lead him to a career. Matt went to the college admissions office and enrolled in the Computer Information Systems degree program. The academic advisor who helped Matt make a course schedule failed to check his entrance exam scores to ensure he was eligible for Composition and Rhetoric and the math courses, all required for program-ready students in the Computer Information Systems program. In addition, Matt requested online courses.

Had the advisor simply checked the entrance test scores, she could have directed Matt to the Learning Support math and English courses which would prepare him to take program courses. Matt's lack of preparation for his classes and his taking online courses, which often offer little student support, meant that he quickly grew frustrated and simply stopped logging on to his math and English courses. He ignored campus emails urging him to drop his courses. The next semester, when his parents took him to enroll for another semester, they learned that Matt was on academic probation because he had failed math and English. His need for Learning Support classes put him behind even further in his program of study.

Shirley is a student in the college Aviation Maintenance Program…

…because it leads to the Airframe and Propulsion (A&P) licensure. The program is certified by the FAA, so it has very strict attendance requirements for the students. The problem is that Shirley is also a member of the Air National Guard and is required to participate in drills during the upcoming semester. (The college instructors had let her know that she must attend each class.) Discouraged with the school's lack of flexibility, she is contemplating dropping out of the Airframe and Propulsion program.

The art of academic advising is mastered using the following five axioms known as the "Five Bs". Every student must:

- ✓ #1 – Be academically prepared for the chosen coursework within a program of study.
- ✓ #2 – Be physically prepared for chosen coursework.
- ✓ #3 – Be financially capable of paying for the chosen coursework.
- ✓ #4 – Be advised with graduation in mind - every semester.
- ✓ #5 – Be registered!

The academic advisor that follows these five axioms is referred to as a *purposeful advisor*.

Each of the previous student situations is real, and each negative outcome could have been avoided if the students' academic advisors had applied the Five Axioms for Purposeful Advisement. The students could have completed their programs successfully. This book is written with Stephanie, Belle, DeShaun, Brian, and Shirley, and too many others in mind.

The academic advisors are college representatives who see each student, one-on-one, each semester. The reason for this individual advising is to ensure that a student is advised with the whole person in mind. That also is the reason the implementation and use of purposeful advisement is important because it considers the whole student, a person with a life, not just a person in classes.

This book gives the academic advisor, a sure and proven method of advisement that makes the students, when they leave, know that they are on the right academic track. They feel nurtured and important. Those who leave the advisor's office with a schedule in hand or those who register themselves online know they will make progress in the next term.

And as you read through this book, think of Stephanie, Belle, DeShaun, Matt, and Shirley and others you might have known. How would this process have prevented their particular outcomes?

Chapter II

Five Axioms for Purposeful Advisement

"Academic advising is the only structured service on the campus in which all students have the opportunity for on-going, one-to-one contact with a concerned representative of the institution."   Dr. Wes Habley

The other day, the air conditioning went out at my house, so I called a local heating and air company to come fix it. After the young man finished his work, he handed me the bill for $752 for replacing the air handler in the attic. I was taken aback at the expense, and instantly I remembered a story Dad told me when I was growing up. It was about a farmer who had a pump go out that provided water to the cattle. The farmer called Old Man Bill's Repairs to send a man to repair the pump.

When old man Bill arrived, the farmer showed him the pump and explained that it didn't work. Old man Bill looked at the pump and said "Hmmm." He retrieved a hammer from his truck, hesitated a moment, then leaned over the pump and gave it one gentle tap with the hammer. The pump started right up and ran perfectly. Old man Bill turned to the farmer and said,

"That will be $101."

"One hundred and one dollars?" exclaimed the farmer. "For what?"

Old man Bill wrote out on the receipt

"One dollar for labor on the pump and one hundred dollars for knowing were to hit it!"

I returned to the moment and asked the air conditioner repair technician where he learned to do his job. He explained that he had graduated from a local technical college. He qualified for a Pell Grant, which paid most of his tuition and fees. Because he had served in the U.S. Marine Corps, his Post-911 GI Bill had covered the rest of his education and living expenses.

The point here is that people take advantage of opportunities at a college, university, community, technical college, and vocational school to acquire valuable knowledge and learn skill sets. However, they need guidance to get into school, navigate successfully through their program of study and have a positive result in the end. Academic advising provides that help.

Purposeful advisors will ensure that students will:

- ✓ #1 – <u>Be academically prepared</u> for the chosen coursework within a program of study.

- ✓ #2 – <u>Be physically prepared</u> for chosen coursework.

- ✓ #3 – <u>Be financially capable</u> of paying for the chosen coursework.

- ✓ #4 – <u>Be advised</u> with graduation in mind - every semester.

- ✓ #5 – <u>Be registered</u>!

Chapter III

To the Reader.

I assume that, as an academic advisor, you have at your college, certain advisement tools at your disposal. Most colleges have software that allows advisors to look at a student's academic history, current status, academic program, and such information as Grade Point Average (GPA) and program courses needed for completion. I refer to these tools as WAAS or Web-Enhanced Academic Advisement Software. The WAAS that I use as an example in this text is DegreeWorks. This software allows advisors to keep notes in the system that record information discussed between advisors and students including recommendations for classes for future terms.

The registrar or academic affairs or student affairs administrator will have the information and training for the system the college uses.

It is also important to note that many of the specific guidelines and recommendations regarding financial aid in this text, though accurate at the time of this publishing, may change as laws and legislators change. The advisor should stay current with applicable federal, state, and institutional guidelines when advising students in the framework and from the scenarios given in this book. It also is important to recognize that each academic institution has its own rules and policies for dropping classes, withdrawal, and other academic activities that can adversely affect a student's academic status.

The Five Axioms:

Every student must:

- ✓ **#1 – Be academically prepared for the chosen coursework within a program of study.**

    #2 – Be physically prepared for chosen coursework.

    #3 – Be financially capable of paying for the chosen coursework.

    #4 – Be advised with graduation in mind - every semester.

    #5 – Be registered!

Academically Prepared

Chapter IV

Axiom #1 - Be academically prepared for the chosen coursework within a program of study.

Every good advisor must become comfortable with the first Axiom that states, "Every student must be academically prepared for the chosen coursework within a program of study." It does not matter whether the student is returning or newly enrolled. First, he/she must have passed the prerequisite class in the previous semester. Second, he/she must have a verified high school diploma to determine academic preparation for college.

Sometimes meeting with the student affords the advisor the opportunity to discuss the need for a GED diploma or perhaps the need for remedial classes available to so many adult learners that have been away from school sometimes for decades. It is also motivating to encourage a student with such comments as, "I see that you passed your last semester classes. Good job!" Reviewing new students' entrance exam scores or the SAT\ACT can open the door for comments such as, "Your test scores are good. You should be ready to go right into your program of study." In case of the need for a remedial course to refresh or relearn math or English skills, the advisor should let the student know at this point and that the college has tutors and learning labs just for that reason. This conversation can set the student at ease and give the advisor the opportunity to show a "can-do" attitude toward the student's future academic success. In other words, every purposeful advisor will assess initially whether students or potential students are prepared for any upcoming coursework.

The purposeful advisor, when advising a currently enrolled student for the next semester, always will find it necessary to review with the student the following from the college's web-based academic advising system (WAAS): 1) Academic Standing, 2) Verify Program of Study, 3) Current GPA, 4) Failed or dropped classes, 5) Needed remedial course based on Entrance\Assessment Test scores. This review shows students that the advisor cares about them and is making sure that they are on track every step of the way each semester. Interestingly, in my experience after this step in the advisement process, the student normally says, "Thank you for looking at this." The purposeful advisor always will make sure that the advisees are academically prepared before letting them register for the subsequent semester courses. It is important in the advisor/student relationship that any issues that directly impact student progress come to the forefront during the advisement session.

One example is noticing in the system or the institutional LMS that there are "holds" on the student's account due to fees or tuition costs that must be paid before registration for the next semester. The advisor has the opportunity at this point to send the student to the applicable office, such as the Business Office or Student Affairs, and address the issue.

One motivator for students in any program is knowing their current Grade Point Average (GPA).

Therefore, the advisor must make sure students know their GPA. "Good" with regards to a GPA sometimes is relative to each individual and the purposeful advisor will take the opportunity to discuss any need for concern. The following chapter provides an example of primary areas that an academic advisor should check and share with the student/advisee. The advisor must make sure students are academically prepared before moving on with their class selection.

Chapter V

Specifics to Check for Academic Preparedness:

Ensure that the student …

- Is in the right program in college's data system

- Passed all classes in the previous semester

- Has taken and passed prerequisite classes

- Has high enough entrance exam scores before placing them in General Education classes.

- Knows the student's academic goal i.e., a certificate, diploma, or degree.

- Doesn't have "holds" on the student account.

- Academic Status is in "Good Standing."

- Knows his/her current GPA.

The Five Axioms:

Every student must:

- ✓ #1 – Be academically prepared for the chosen coursework within a program of study.

- ✓ **#2 – Be physically prepared for chosen coursework.**

    #3 – Be financially capable of paying for the chosen coursework.

    #4 – Be advised with graduation in mind - every semester.

    #5 – Be registered!

ℙ

Physically Prepared

Chapter VI

Axiom #2 – Be Physically Prepared

Students entering vocational education come from all backgrounds, and many have challenges that make attending classes physically difficult. Some take the bus, the subway, or other form of mass transit. There are also the challenges that students with special needs face and the provisions under the Americans with Disabilities Act. The advisor must be mindful of these issues and so many more when purposefully advising students. For example, a student who arrives for advisement wearing military fatigues likely will have military maneuvers that could impact her attendance in her program of study. A purposeful advisor would refer her to the Veteran's Affairs office for more direct guidance with regards to military orders and enrollment. A student interested in a program offered only on a satellite campus in another town might face a challenge of transportation needs.

A question that I often get when speaking with advisors and administrators alike is the issue facing the advisor of multi-campus program offerings. A student or parent may ask whether we offer a certain course of study at "the college". The answer to this question is more than a simple "yes" or "no". The answer should include where, geographically, courses are being taught. Colleges today often are spread out over vast regions of the city, state, country, and the world if taught online. It is embarrassing to advise, register, and provide a schedule printout to a student only to have the student look at it and say, "Oh, I don't have a car, and I can't take classes on a campus thirty miles from here." or "You put me in online classes, and I don't have a computer or access to the internet."

Academic advisors want to be ever mindful of the student's physical capabilities associated with taking classes at the college. This is a good point in the advisement process to share a list of resources that the college has to offer a diverse student population.

Chapter VI provides an example of primary areas to which an academic advisor would refer the advisee enrolled in any program of study at the specific institution of higher learning. These areas pertain to a student's being physically prepared for classes to start that semester.

Chapter VII

Check for Physical Preparedness

Ensure that the student ...

- Has a computer or access to one.

- Is physically capable of attending to classes at the applicable campus and at that time.

- Knows about the available student services including:

    o Clubs and student organizations.

    o Tutors and tutoring centers on campus.

    o Veteran's Affairs

    o Federal and state assistance programs like REACH, WIOA, Special Populations, etc.

    o Campus maps

    o Common and useful areas of the college website

The Five Axioms:

Every student must:

- ✓ #1 – Be academically prepared for the chosen coursework within a program of study.

- ✓ #2 – Be physically prepared for chosen coursework.

- ✓ **#3 – Be financially capable of paying for the chosen coursework.**

    #4 – Be advised with graduation in mind - every semester.

    #5 – Be registered!

$

Financially Prepared

Chapter VIII

Axiom #3 – Be financially capable of paying...

(Probably the most important Axiom!)

For students entering most academic programs, the issues of financial aid and how to pay for classes, books, and supplies are paramount. A key element in the art of advising students each semester is in keeping them in good standing with their financial aid. Telling students up front that dropping classes before a certain point in the semester or failing classes can cost them their financial aid will better prepare them for the road ahead. Academic advisors normally are not expected to be the experts on financial aid, but they need to remind their advisees of a handful of important points each semester. The purposeful advisor should know State and institutional policies regarding financial aid programs. They should understand GPA and attempted-hours requirements that affect financial aid as well as criteria for academic probation. One of the most common issues in the classroom in the first few days of each semester is that of students' not having their books and supplies because of delayed financial aid.

The advisor should remind advisees to have FAFSA forms completed and submitted far enough in advance of classes to be able to get through the bookstore without problems. Normally, student advisement occurs early enough before the next semester for students to be able to check with the campus Financial Aid Office.

The following chapter provides an example of specific points that purposeful advisors should share with advisees pertaining to student financial aid. This can keep the students financially capable of paying for coursework.

Chapter IX

Specific Points of Financial Preparedness

I recognize that each state has its own rules governing student academic performance and financial aid status. Here is an example of key points that I find useful in the advisement process. Recognizing that I'm not a financial aid expert, the experts gave me these points to cover...

Ensure that the student...

- Has submitted the FAFSA before the semester starts so money is available to purchase books and supplies for classes.

- Knows that dropping or failing classes can affect financial aid.

- Knows that dropping classes before midterm can have certain consequences.

- Knows how to access the college's financial aid website

- Knows financial aid deadlines (often on the website)

Here are some important federal regulations that I read to advisees each semester:

1. To maintain good academic standing and Student Academic Progress (SAP), student must have a minimum GPA of 2.0 AND a successful attempt rate of 67%.

2. Dropping a class after the drop\add period but before midterm results in a grade of W which does not affect GPA but does affect successful attempted hours.

3. Dropping a class after midterm results in a grade of either a WP or a WF. The grade of WP counts toward successfully attempted hours but not GPA. The grade of WF negatively affects both GPA and attempted hours.

4. Pell/Loan recipients who drop a class before the 60% point of the semester will have to pay back the unearned portion of their Pell/Loan awards.

The Five Axioms:

Every student must:

- ✓ #1 – Be academically prepared for the chosen coursework within a program of study.

- ✓ #1 – Be physically prepared for chosen coursework.

- ✓ #3 – Be financially capable of paying for the chosen coursework.

- ✓ **#4 – Be advised with graduation in mind - every semester.**

    #5 – Be registered!

A
-
Advised

Chapter X

Axion #4 – Be advised with graduation in mind - Every time!

"Begin with the end in mind." - Stephen R. Covey

One evening, I was talking to my son-in-law about how his studies were going at the university he was attending. I asked when he would be completing his program so we can make plans to attend his graduation. He told me he had no idea when he would be done. He seemed confused about what classes had transferred in from other colleges and what classes he needed next. What should have been a simple question leading to a simple answer led to a realization that this young man had not been properly advised in some time. The art of academic advising is anchored to the student's graduation date. Whether an advisor is advising a medical student in the last semester clinicals or a welding student with one class left in the program is irrelevant. If a student is missing a required English or math class and the advisor fails to advise accordingly, then neither will graduate. This is what advising with graduation in mind means.

A purposeful advisor will always check the student history of courses taken in a program. Then the advisor can project program completion for the student. The next step is to recommend classes for the coming semester and entering the recommendation into the "Notes" section of the WAAS.

One final note: A student completing courses of instruction needs to look at graduation requirements and prepare to apply for graduation. Students do not necessarily know what to do to graduate. One final note: An important part of Axiom #4 is *documentation*!

In most web-based academic advising systems (WAAS) a "Notes" section allows the advisor to record and save what the conversation with the student including any issues that arise at the time of advisement. This provides documentation for the student to review when accessing the WAAS and safeguards the advisor in situations of student appeals or questions of what the advisee was told at the time of the advisement.

The Five Axioms:

Every student must:

- ✓ #1 – Be academically prepared for the chosen coursework within a program of study.

- ✓ #2 – Be physically prepared for chosen coursework.

- ✓ #3 – Be financially capable of paying for the chosen coursework.

- ✓ #4 – Be advised with graduation in mind - every semester.

- ✓ **#5 – Be registered!**

Ř - Register

Chapter XI

Axion #5 – Be Registered!

"A student can be registered and not properly advised, but a student cannot be properly advised and not registered"

Few things in life are more fulfilling to students than the knowledge that have registered successfully for the next semester's classes. They all know that someone is going to ask, "Hey, are you registered?" Being able to answer positively can make their day. Having touched base on their class history, made sure they can take and pay for the classes, and advised on the appropriate classes towards finishing the program, the advisor can register students or have them register themselves.

Having completed "The Five Bs," the advisor should provide the student with a paper copy of the schedule. If the student registered their self then still offer to print out their schedule. It makes the student feel whole! At the point in the advisement process, I always remind the advisee that dates of the drop/add period normally are emailed to students at the beginning of each semester. The student should check email at least a couple of times each week for updates from the college or university.

Part Two: Academic Advising Scenarios

Chapter XII

Scenario #1

Advising One-On-One (No Issues)

Advisor: Hey, What's up?

Student: Can you register me?

Advisor: I can and will (we laugh). Have a seat. What is your Student ID number?

Student: It's 910XXXXX

Advisor: Let me look at your history in the system. (DegreeWorks or another one of many WAAS)

> You are Frank N. Stein, right? (He nods nervously)
>
> I see you are in the Engineering Technology track.
>
> Your GPA is currently 4.0.
>
> You have no "holds" on your account.
>
> There are no embedded certificate programs in this track.
>
> Looks like you passed your classes last semester. Good Job!

Let's look at the classes offered on the college website and at your program of study to see what you want to take next.

Student: I'll take these classes right here. (He points to four classes on my computer screen)

Advisor: Great choice! Those classes are the next ones for your program! So, I'll advise you to take ENGT 11XX, ENGT 11XX, PSYCH 1101 and the next ENGL 1102 course. This will keep you on track to graduate on schedule for a second-semester

Engineering Technology student. So, I'll type those classes into the Notes section in the system (DegreeWorks is the WAAS that I use.). You will be able to access this DegreeWorks sheet in your Student Portal. This way, you and I can both keep track of what you are advised to take. How does that sound to you?

Student: No Way!!! That's great…Thanks!

Advisor: That's a good schedule. The college also has some amazing student services, clubs and organizations, and even an Academic Success Center to help you in many areas of life including tutoring if you need it. Let me email you, at your student email account, a list of links of services the college provides through our Student Life and Student Services. (Email a list applicable to the institution.)

Student: That's great to have especially in celebrating diversity with other students.

Advisor: OK…let's talk about financial aid. If you decide to drop a class or classes, make sure to do it during the drop\add period at the beginning of the semester. Let me take a few seconds to read you some points to remember: (Read these.)

> 1. If you drop any class after the drop\add period but before midterm you will receive a "W" on your transcripts. This will not affect your GPA but will count as attempted hours.

If you drop a class after midterm you will get either a Withdraw Fail\WF or a Withdraw Passing\WP depending on your grades in the class at the time.

2. A grade of WF counts against your GPA and "attempted hours."

3. A Grade of WP doesn't affect your GPA but does count against your attempted hours.

4. Make sure your FAFSA is up-to-date so you will not lose your financial aid going into next semester when you need to pay for your books, tuition and fees.

Student: All of that stuff is done already.

Advisor: Cool, let's get you registered for those classes. (I bring up my registration screen and register him for his classes.)

Student: Can I get a copy of my schedule? My parents are going to need it for their insurance.

Advisor: Good job! I'll print out your schedule. (It prints, and I hand it to the student.) Oh, check your email a few times per week. That's how the college keeps you in the loop on deadlines especially with regards to financial aid.

Student: Thank you so much.

Chapter XIII

Scenario #2

Advising One-On-One – Failed MATH 1111

Advisor: Hey, May I help you?

Student: Yes…I need to get registered for next semester.

Advisor: I can certainly advise you. Have a seat. What is your Student ID number?

Student: It's 910XXXXX

Advisor: Let me look at your history in the system. (DegreeWorks or another one of many WAAS)

    You are Jane Doe, right? (She nods and laughs)

    I see you are in the Engineering Technology track.

    Your GPA is currently 3.17.

    You have no "holds" on your account.

Advisor (cont'd): There are no embedded Certificate Programs in this track.

Looks like you passed your English 1101 class last semester but failed your college algebra, MATH 1111 class. Tell me about that math class.

Student: Yeah, that math class was horrible, and I didn't like the professor. Can I take it online and from another professor? I could have used a tutor.

Advisor: Sure, you can take the online MATH 1111 course. The college also has some amazing student services, clubs and organizations, and even an Academic Success Center to help you in many areas of life including tutoring in math.

Advisor (cont'd): Let me email you at your student email account a list of links of services the college provides through our Student Life and Student Services. (Email her a list applicable to your institution)

Student: That's great. Can I retake MATH 1111 along with the next classes I need to finish my program and still be on track?

Advisor: Yes. Let's look at the classes offered on the college website and look at your program of study and see what you want to take next. (The student looks at her iPad and picks the four classes that follow in the sequence for her program.)

Student: I'll take these classes right here. (She points to four classes)

Advisor: OK, great, those classes are the next ones for your program! I'll advise you to take ENGT 11XX, ENGT 11XX, your MATH 1111 again, and the next ENGL 1102 course. This will keep you on track to graduate on schedule for a second-semester Engineering Technology student.

So, I'll type those classes into the Notes section in the system (DegreeWorks is the WAAS that I use.). You will be able to access this DegreeWorks sheet in your Student Portal. This way you and I can both keep track of what you are advised to take. I also put in the Notes that you asked to retake the MATH 1111 class online this time. How does that sound to you?

Student: Great…Thanks!

Advisor: OK...let's talk about Financial Aid. If you decide to drop classes, make sure to do it during the drop\add period at the beginning of the semester. Let me take a few seconds to read you some points to remember: (Read these)

1. If you drop any class after the drop\add period but before midterm you will receive a "W" on your transcripts. This will not affect your GPA but will count as attempted hours.

2. If you drop a class after midterm you will get either a Withdraw Fail\WF or a Withdraw Passing\WP depending on your grades in the class at the time.

3. A grade of WF counts against your GPA and attempted hours.

4. A grade of WP doesn't affect your GPA but does count against your attempted hours.

5. Make sure your FAFSA is up-to-date so you don't lose your financial aid going into next semester when you need to pay for your books, tuition and fees.

Student: My mom usually makes sure all of that is taken care of.

Advisor: OK, I'm just touching base on it because it's important. Now let's get you registered for those classes.

Student: I'll register using my iPad. (She registers herself.) I see those classes you advised me to take. Ok…I'm done…. registered! Awesome!

Advisor: Good job! I'll print out your schedule. (It prints, and I hand it to the student.) Oh, check your email a few times per week. That's how the college keeps you in the loop on deadlines especially with regards to financial aid.

Student: Thank you so much.

Advisor: Glad I could help.

Chapter XIV

Scenario #3

Advising an Online Student

Advisor: Email the following:

Advisement Email – Read Carefully

Dear Joe Schmoe – Student ID #910XXXXXX

It's time for advisement for next semester.

I see you are in the Engineering Technology track.

Your GPA is currently 4.0.

You have no "holds" on your account.

There are no embedded certificate programs in this track.

Looks like you passed your classes last semester. Good Job!

Let's look at the classes offered on the college website for your program of study. I'm advising you to take ENGT 11XX, ENGT 11XX, PSYCH 1101 and the next ENGL 1102 course.

This will keep you on track to graduate on schedule for a second-semester Engineering Technology student. So, I'll type those classes into the Notes section in the system (DegreeWorks is the WAAS that I use.). You will be able to access this DegreeWorks sheet in your Student Portal. This way, you and I can both keep track of what you are advised to take. Email me back if there are any questions about these classes.

You have a good schedule. The college also has some amazing student services, clubs and organizations, and even an Academic Success Center to help you in many areas of life including tutoring if you need it. I have attached a list of links of services the college provides through our Student Life and Student Services.

OK…About financial aid. If you decide to drop classes, make sure to do it during the drop\add period at the beginning of the semester. Because financial aid is important to you, I want to focus on that area.

Let me draw your attention to some important points to remember:

- If you drop any class after the drop\add period but before midterm you will receive a "W" on your transcripts. This will not affect your GPA but will count as attempted hours.

- If you drop a class after midterm you will receive either a Withdraw Fail\WF or a Withdraw Passing\WP depending on your grades in the class at the time.

- A grade of WF counts against your GPA and attempted hours.

- A Grade of WP doesn't affect your GPA but does count against your attempted hours.

- Make sure your FAFSA is up-to-date so you don't lose your financial aid going into next semester when you need to pay for your books, tuition and fees.

You can register for the advised classes or contact me, and I can register you. <u>Email me back</u> when you are registered so I can know you are good-to-go.

Feel free to contact me at any time via email or phone at (XXX) XXX-XXXX or come by my office.

(Email the student the DegreeWorks sheet with Notes)

Chapter XV

Scenario #4

Advising a Student with "Undecided Major"

Student: I need to be advised, can you help me?

Advisor: Sure. What's your Student ID number?

Student: It's 910XXXXX.

(Advisor enters number into the system.)

Advisor: Okay, here we go. Your name is Jerry Fusmucker, right?

Student: Yes, but you can call me Fuss.

Advisor: All right Fuss, I see that you are designated in the system as "undecided" for a major.

Student: Yeah, I'm not sure what I want to major in. I'm thinking either biology or history.

Advisor: Your current GPA after two semesters is 2.8. You failed your college algebra class your first semester and took it again this semester with a different professor. How is it going now?

Student: I have a high B in her class right now, and she's very helpful.

Advisor: Good work. Keep it up. Let's look at what core academic classes you still need regardless of what major you end up selecting. Let's look at getting you into your next math class, ENGL 1102, PSYC 1101, and BIOL 1101. That will get you over the halfway point in your core classes. How does that sound?

Student: That's great. Let me register myself for those classes really quick.

Advisor: Before you do that, you should know that the college also has some amazing student services, clubs and organizations, and even an Academic Success Center to help you in many areas of life including tutoring if you need it. Let me email you, at your student email account, a list of links of services the college provides through our Student Life and Student Services. (Email a list applicable to your institution.)

Advisor: OK…let's talk about financial aid. If you decide to drop classes, make sure to do it during the drop\add period at the beginning of the semester.

Let me take a few seconds to read you some points to remember: (Read these)

1. If you drop any class after the drop\add period but before midterm you will receive a "W" on your transcripts. This will not affect your GPA but will count as "Attempted Hours."

2. If you drop a class after midterm you will get either a Withdraw Fail\WF or a Withdraw Passing\WP depending on your grades in the class at the time.

(Read These -cont'd)

3. A grade of WF counts against your GPA and "attempted hours."

4. A Grade of WP doesn't affect your GPA but does count against your attempted hours.

5. Make sure your FAFSA is up-to-date so you don't lose your financial aid going into next semester when you need to pay for your books, tuition and fees.

Student: I'm not using federal funds for my college. My folks are paying for my classes.

Advisor: Why don't you go ahead while we're sitting here and register for your classes, so we can make sure all goes well.

Student: Sure. I'll put the course numbers in right here and…Okay…there! I'm registered. Thanks.

Advisor: Awesome! Just a reminder to check your email a few times per week. That's how the college keeps you in the loop on college activities that you might need to know about. And start thinking about choosing a major by the time we meet next semester for advisement. Nice to meet you, Fuss!

Student: Thank you so much and nice to meet you too!

Part Three:

Questions on Purposeful Academic Advising

Chapter XVI

Question #1 - How long does it normally take an advisor to go through all these points with a student?

Answer: Anyone who advises students realizes that the process can take any amount of time. Proper and purposeful advising doesn't add much to that process. Just last week, I had a colleague sit in on a random advisement session with a student who had a couple of issues with regards to his next semester classes. I went through the five axioms, and he walked away from me with a schedule and registered for classes. The colleague said, "That was fascinating to watch. By the way…it took thirteen minutes start to finish". The factor that normally takes the most time is advising students on what core classes to take or at some other point at which they are indecisive.

Chapter XVII

Question #2 - Do program advisors have to advise the same way that academic advisors in Student Services do?

Answer: All students are to be advised the same proper and purposeful way. Granted, program advisors will have a better understanding of sequences of certain classes that might benefit the student, but all students need to have all five "Bs" addressed.

Chapter XVIII

Question #3 - Isn't vocational or technical college student advisement different from liberal arts college student advisement?

Answer: No. Students enrolling in any type of postsecondary education program need their academic advisor to review their previous course history and test scores to make sure they are ready to move on to the next set of required courses for their program. Every student needs to be reminded that there are support systems (student organizations, clubs, tutors, etc.) at the college to help students along the path to successful completion of their course of instruction.

Every student needs to be reminded of points in student\academic life that can directly affect financial aid. All students at either a vocational\technical or liberal arts college need the advisement recommendations noted in the advisement software system. The notes are especially important points when they reflect whether a student asks to take a class online previously failed when the advisor suggested that it be taken in the classroom. Lastly, all students need to be registered during advisement. Some students want to register themselves, and some want the advisor to do it. Some institutions do not give advisors permission to register students. In such situations, the advisor should have a computer with the internet is nearby to be able to verify that the student is actually registered for classes when they leave advisement. I will acknowledge that some students can take care of their own registration and need little or no assistance in the advisement process regardless of the college they attend. However, students are students and the academic advisors are the professionals.

Chapter XIX

Question #4 - Isn't this all supposed to be covered in new-student orientation?

Answer: Yes and No – But more No than Yes! A new-student orientation will cover many topics that relate to the academic success of a student: A tour of the campus, speakers from Student Services\Affairs discussing financial aid, and various programs and organizations designed to improve student life, etc. What it doesn't do is look at whether an advisee passed last semester's ENGL 1101 allowing her to move on to ENGL 1102.

New-student orientation doesn't recommend what course students need to take in order to finish their chosen program of study in a timely manner nor does it register students or ensure that they are properly advised for classes.

Let's be honest; do any of us really remember all of the "important stuff" we heard at new-student orientation of freshman year in college? Purposeful advisement touches on key points each semester during the advisement session to help students avoid obstacles to their academic success.

Chapter XX

Question #5 - Where can I find more resources and organizations that I can contact for more information about other aspects of academic advisement?

Answer: There are many resources available on the internet on academic advising. For those inclined to scholarly research and excellent writing on the academic side of advising, I find that one of the best is the NACADA website at https://www.nacada.ksu.edu/. National **A**cademic **AD**vising Association- The Global Community of Academic Advisors is a tremendous organization of professionals from all around the world each working to make academic advising better for their students.

The organization is housed at Kansas State University in Manhattan, Kansas, and the website has a ton of great books and research material and one of the best journals in the field – The NADACA Journal.

In addition to the very good resources referenced above is the academic advisement program used at Central Georgia Technical College (CGTC) with campuses all over Middle Georgia. This college uses the framework of the Five-Axioms in *The Art of Academic Advising* in the form of the ALFAA 5-Step Advisement Process. ALFAA is an acronym which stands for **A**-Academic Preparedness, **L** – Life Challenges, **F** – Financial, **A** – Advise for classes, and **A** – Affirm Registration.

This college has an ALFAA Checklist on its website that all advisors follow for advising students. Advisors then send the list of all-important links to student email accounts for future reference to available resources and reminders. An example of a successfully executed advisement plan is in Chapter XXI–Exhibit A.

Reference:

Central Georgia Technical College. (2015). *Addressing the ALFAA Bs – Identifying Barriers and setting Benchmarks through Purposeful Advising.*

Chapter XXI

*Exhibit A**

Central Georgia Technical College
Five-Step ALFAA Advisement Plan

ALFAA Advisement Sheet

This is a simple five-step advisement process, referred to by the acronym – ALFAA, each letter coinciding with the steps as seen below. The ALFAA process has been designed and developed with the direct input from CGTC faculty, staff, and students to aid academic advisors in advising students in an efficient and thorough manner. The ALFAA five-step process addresses barriers that have been challenges to our students' academic success. The plan will help them meet the benchmarks set for finishing their program as quickly as possible.

Student Information Student ID

Central Georgia Technical College

ALFAA Step 1: Academic Preparedness

Check for the following in DegreeWorks:

Review academic history to determine if the student has been set up for success.

Check the following on the DegreeWorks sheet with advisee:

- Major and assigned advisor
- Enrollment status (actively enrolled)
- GPA
- Academic status (SAP) - warning, probation, or suspension
- Learning support (remedial)
- Student passed prior classes
- Graduation ready - diploma/degree

Log-In from BannerWeb to continue to DegreeWorks: CLICK HERE

Course delivery preferences face-to-face, hybrid, BlendFlex, and online classes.

Does the student match the program?

Acknowledge embedded TCCs

Official Academic Calendar

Central Georgia Technical College

ALFAA Step 2: Life Challenges

Military members called to be deployed must provide military orders to be allowed to drop classes without penalty (no impact on GPA or successful attempt rate).

Remind student of the various student organizations.

Make student aware of the various services available:

- Academic Success Center (Tutoring)
- New Student Orientation Handbook
- Care Center (Advising)
- Tuition and Textbook Scholarships
- REACH Mentoring Organization
- Special Populations
- TEAMS (early alert)
- Military and Veteran Services
- On-campus Child Development Centers

Central Georgia Technical College
ALFAA Step 2: Life Challenges - Continued

Share Catalog Link:
http://www.centralgatech.edu/catalog

Share Campus Map Link:
http://www.centralgatech.edu/about-cgtc/campuses-and-centers/

Share Directory of College Departments

WIOA Program

New Student "How-To" Videos

- How to Register for Classes
- How to Withdraw/ Drop Classes

Central Georgia Technical College

ALFAA Step 3: Financial

<u>Financial Aid office</u>

<u>Important Financial Aid Deadlines</u> - If all financial aid documents (FAFSA), normally completed once per calendar year, are not received and processed by the the first day of school, the aid/book voucher will not be ready for purchasing books and supplies.

Dropping a class may impact financial aid.

To maintain good academic standing and Student Academic Progress (SAP), student must have a minimum GPA of 2.0 AND a successful attempt rate of 67%.

Dropping a class after the drop/add period but before midterm results in a grade of W, which does not affect GPA, but does affect successful attempted hours.

Dropping a class after midterm results in a grade of either a WP or a WF. The grade of WP counts toward successfully attempted hours but not GPA. The grade of WF affects both GPA and attempted hours.

Pell/Loan recipients who drop a class before the 60% point of the semester will have to pay the unearned portion of their Pell/Loan awards back.

Explain the impact of outstanding balance paid for courses (the Purge).

Central Georgia Technical College

ALFAA Step 4: Advise for classes

For distance-education students, explain different delivery methods (face-to-face, online, hybrid, telepresence) and direct them to website resources.

Advise for graduation, not just the next semester's classes. Log in from BannerWeb to continue to DegreeWorks.

Taking more than 15 credit hours each semester improves program completion time (15 to Finish)

Make sure students can access their CGTC email account. (Technology Instructions- How to set up student email on a smart phone)

DegreeWorks Notes section for current semester advisement entered.

Student is now advised but NOT registered!

Central Georgia Technical College

ALFAA Step 5: Affirm Purposeful Advisement

Provide information and/or assistance to register through BannerWeb.

Register student in Banner or have student register on another computer and send Registration Letter/Instructions to student.

Remind students of drop/add and refund procedures and deadlines.

Remind students of attendance requirements

☑ I have reviewed the information above with the student.

*The information in this exhibit is reformatted from the Central Georgia Technical College ALFAA Sheet which is a checklist in HTML used by all academic advisors. This exhibit is used with permission from CGTC.

Chapter XXII

Addressing the Horror Stories

Let's return to the foundational principles in the *Art of Academic Advisement.* The Five Axioms or **Five – Be's** state that every student must…

1) **Be** <u>academically prepared</u> for the chosen coursework within a program of study;

2) **Be** <u>physically prepared</u> for chosen coursework;

3) **Be** <u>financially capable</u> of paying for the chosen coursework;

4) **Be** <u>advised with graduation in mind – every</u> semester.

5 – **Be** <u>registered</u>!

Let's see…

how would the artful use of purposeful advisement have handled the important student scenarios of Stephanie the nursing student, DeShaun the cosmetology major, Belle the poly sci major, Matt the online student, and Shirley the Aircraft Maintenance student serving in the military? Could the advisor have prevented the horrible results of each of these scenarios by properly advising the students? I say yes! Let's evaluate each situation through the lens of *purposeful advisement*.

Stephanie, a pre-nursing student, ...

was scheduled for too many classes, could not handle the course load, and failed one of those classes – a required core course for the program she wants. The real problem is that admission to the nursing program is competitive. Failing that class lowered her GPA and hurt any chance she had of getting into the nursing program. This scenario is devastating to any student, and Stephanie dropped out of the college.

Axiom #4 – Advising with graduation in mind might have prevented Stephanie's scenario from becoming a horror story. Looking at her situation and course sequence, her advisor would have recognized that overloading a nursing student in her core academic classes when a higher GPA is the desired goal is a not a good idea.

DeShaun is a cosmetology major…

in his first semester courses. On the first day of the semester, the instructor told the class that each student needed an additional mannequin kit for his class. At the bookstore, DeShaun learned that he didn't have any financial aid from which to purchase it. He dropped the class because he didn't have the funds to buy the $200 cosmetology kit. This put him off-track to finish his program in a timely manner as the classes were setup in a certain sequence.

In DeShaun's case, consider the importance of the advisor's simply following the guidance of Axiom #3 - Be financially capable of paying for the chosen coursework. What could the impact have been on DeShaun if he had been told to walk over to the Financial Aid Office to make sure his financial aid was ready to go for the following semester? That act alone could have meant the difference between his staying in school and dropping out.

Belle, a political science major…

in her sophomore year, lacked confidence in her math skills. Because she felt that she had no one to turn to, she failed. Belle was devastated because failing this class dropped her GPA below the requirement for her scholarship. The sad part of this scenario is that the tutoring center was next door to her dorm. Had her advisor told about these available student services, she could have gotten the help she needed with her math. Axiom #2 says that the students should be physically prepared for chosen coursework.

Colleges provide clubs, student organizations, tutoring centers and other services to be physically located for the student's convenience. It should also be noted that part of a student's financial readiness in Axiom #3 is for the advisor to show the students where they can find information on scholarships available to the college. Perhaps this could have given Belle more options than the one scholarship she had and lost.

Matt is an online student...

with an academic advisor who advised Matt without checking his entrance exam scores to see if Matt had scored high enough to take English Composition and Rhetoric and math classes, two of the program-ready core academic classes for his program. Matt asked if he could take the classes online, and the advisor said that he could. If Matt's advisor had followed the first step in purposeful advisement Axiom #1 – Be academically prepared – he would have checked test scores to see if Matt needed Learning Support\Remedial courses. Of course, academic advisors ae not to blame when students stop doing their coursework and refuse to respond to an instructor's emails. What advisors should do is ensure that a student is academically ready to take classes, especially in the case of online classes that require self-discipline.

And then there is *Shirley in the Aviation Maintenance Program…*

that leads to the Airframe and Propulsion (A&P) licensure. Because the program is certified by the FAA, it has very strict attendance requirements for the students. The problem is that Shirley also is a member of the Air National Guard and has required drills scheduled during the coming semester. Another good aspect of Axiom #2 is that it gives the advisor the opportunity to refer students in military service and those needing assistance in Veteran's Affairs to the link on the college website for the policies regarding students with military orders. The fact that instructors are telling Shirley that she is required to be in class during all class times based on the FAA regulations means that she, with her advisor, will need to consider carefully all options for program completion.

Axiom #5 stating that students should be registered before leaving the advisement session did not play a role in the horror stories of Stephanie, Belle, DeShaun, Matt, and Shirley. It is part of *The Art of Academic Advising* because it seals the deal and gives the students closure and assurance that they are ready for the following semester. A student should never think that being told what to register for constitutes actual registration. There's not much in life that makes students happier than having their schedule for the next semester in their hand. (Exaggeration, don't you think?) Remember – They take it to class the first day of each semester!

Epilogue

Thank you for reading this book. Now, take the Five-Step Process of Purposeful Advisement and make each Axiom paramount to improving our students' academic success and increasing the colleges' retention. Those who seriously and consciously apply the principles in this book will truly practice the *Art of Academic Advisement.*

About the Author

Jeffrey C. Hoffman's experience in academic advising spans over fifteen years in postsecondary education following his over twenty years in military training and an exciting career in the United States Navy's Nuclear Submarine Force. His doctoral research centered on technical college student motivation using Vroom's expectancy theory. Jeff served as Director of Instruction at Coastal Pines Technical College and Chairman of the Quality Enhancement Plan Steering Committee at Central Georgia Technical College (CGTC) in Warner Robins, Georgia. His Five-Step Process for Purposeful Advisement is the model for the college's ALFAA Advisement Process. Jeff served as Aerospace, Trade, and Industry – Technical Division Head at CGTC until 2018. Currently, he works for the Department of Defense.

☐

Feel free to share any and all correspondence via email to drjeffhoffman62@gmail.com.

Made in the USA
Monee, IL
13 January 2020